CR

INDIANA
HOOSIERS

BY DREW SILVERMAN

Published by ABDO Publishing Company, PO Box 398166, Minneapolis, MN 55439. Copyright © 2014 by Abdo Consulting Group, Inc. International copyrights reserved in all countries. No part of this book may be reproduced in any form without written permission from the publisher. SportsZone™ is a trademark and logo of ABDO Publishing Company.

Printed in the United States of America,
North Mankato, Minnesota
072013
092013

 THIS BOOK CONTAINS AT LEAST 10% RECYCLED MATERIALS.

Editor: Chrös McDougall
Series Designer: Craig Hinton

Photo Credits: Susan Regan/AP Images, cover; Bob Jordan/AP Images, 1; AP Images, 4, 7, 9, 11, 17, 18, 21, 42 (top), 43 (top left), 43 (top right); Archive Image/Alamy, 12; Larry Stoddard/AP Images, 23, 42 (bottom left); Bill Ingraham/AP Images, 25; Fred Jewell/AP Images, 26; Ron Heflin/AP Images, 29, 30, 42 (bottom right); South Bend Tribune, Jim Rider/AP Images, 33; Bloomington Herald-Times, Jeremy Hogan, 34; Dave Martin/AP Images, 37, 43 (bottom); Jeff Roberson/AP Images, 38; Al Behrman/AP Images, 41; Cal Sports Media via AP Images, 44

Design elements: Matthew Brown/iStockphoto

Library of Congress Control Number: 2013938130

Cataloging-in-Publication Data
Silverman, Drew, 1982-
 Indiana Hoosiers / Drew Silverman.
  p. cm. -- (Inside college basketball)
Includes index.
ISBN 978-1-61783-915-3
1. Indiana University, Bloomington--Basketball--Juvenile literature. 2. Indiana Hoosiers (Basketball team)--Juvenile literature. I. Title.
796.323--dc23

                                                              2013938130

TABLE OF CONTENTS

Indiana's Scott May cuts down the net after the Hoosiers' 1976 NCAA championship win over Michigan.

THE PERFECT SEASON

O NE BY ONE, THE INDIANA UNIVERSITY HOOSIERS' STAR PLAYERS CAME OFF THE COURT. THEY WERE SMILING, DANCING, AND HUGGING EACH OTHER. THEY WERE ABOUT TO BECOME CHAMPIONS.

First it was Quinn Buckner. Then it was Scott May. And then came Kent Benson. As the seconds ticked down in the 1976 National Collegiate Athletic Association (NCAA) championship game, Indiana coach Bobby Knight gave each player a meaningful hug. His team was about to defeat the Michigan Wolverines to win the national title. But Knight and the Hoosiers were not only celebrating a championship. They were celebrating perfection.

The 86–68 victory over Michigan completed an undefeated season for Indiana. The 1975–76 Hoosiers played 32 games, and they won all 32. Through the 2012–13 season, no other men's Division I team has had a perfect season since.

Knight was just 35 years old, and it was only his fifth season as Indiana's coach. However, his team was an experienced group. The starting lineup featured four seniors and one junior.

Bob Wilkerson was the senior point guard. Buckner, another senior, joined him in the backcourt. Both starting forwards were seniors. May averaged 23.5 points and 7.7 rebounds per game that season. Tom Abernethy, the other starting forward, scored an average of 10 points per game. Benson was the only non-senior starter. The junior center averaged 17.3 points and 8.8 rebounds per game.

Expectations were high from the start. The Hoosiers had gone 31–1 the previous year. Most of their key players were back in 1975–76. So the team began the season ranked number one in the country.

The day before practice started in 1975, Knight delivered a message to his players. He told them that it would not be enough to win the Big Ten Conference title. It would not even be enough to win the NCAA Tournament. "You beat everybody that we play," Knight told his team.

WORLD BEATERS

Leading up to the 1975–76 season, Indiana played an exhibition game against the Soviet Union national team. Many of the Soviet players remained from the squad that won an Olympic gold medal in 1972. The Soviets were still considered the best amateur team in the world. Yet they were no match for the Hoosiers. Indiana defeated the Soviets 94–78. Scott May made 13 of the 15 shots he attempted. He did not miss a shot in the second half. May finished with 34 points in the convincing win.

Senior forward Scott May was a key player for the Indiana Hoosiers in 1975–76.

And so they did, beginning with the defending NCAA champions. The University of California, Los Angeles (UCLA) Bruins were ranked second in the country. They had won the national championship in 1975. In fact, they had won 10 of the previous 12 NCAA titles. But on this day, the Hoosiers dominated them in an 84–64 Indiana win.

Indiana headed into Big Ten play with a 9–0 record. Its first conference game was against the Ohio State Buckeyes. It would be the closest game the Hoosiers played all season. However, they survived the Buckeyes, winning 66–64. Indiana then went on to finish 18–0 in the Big Ten for the second straight season. That added up to an undefeated 27–0 regular season.

Next up was the NCAA Tournament. Indiana began against the St. John's Redmen. Earlier in the season, the Hoosiers had struggled in a seven-point win over the Redmen. But this time, May scored 33 points as Indiana cruised to a 90–70 victory.

The Alabama Crimson Tide played Indiana tough in the second round. Alabama even led 69–68 with a little more than two minutes to play. But then the Hoosiers clamped down on defense. May put the Hoosiers ahead with a 17-foot jump shot with 2:02 remaining. He had 25 points and 16 rebounds in the 74–69 win.

That victory set up a showdown between number one and number two. Top-ranked Indiana was 29–0 on the season. The second-ranked Marquette Warriors were 27–1. Only one could go on to the Final Four,

BIG TEN PERFECTION

In the first 100 years of the Big Ten Conference, through 2004–05, only twice did a school sweep its league schedule. In other words, only twice did a team win every game it played against its conference opponents—both at home and on the road. Those two teams were Indiana in 1974–75 and Indiana again in 1975–76.

however. The game was close throughout. Indiana led just 57–54 with 25 seconds remaining. But six late free throws by Indiana and a last-second layup by Buckner provided the final margin in a 65–56 Indiana victory.

"It was the type of game true championship teams win," said Marquette coach Al McGuire.

The Hoosiers were heading back to the Final Four for only the third time. Awaiting them was a rematch against UCLA. Benson got in early foul trouble against the Bruins. But Abernethy came up big

THE PERFECT SEASON

WELL RECOGNIZED

The Hoosiers received several major awards during the 1975–76 season. Bobby Knight was chosen as the consensus National Coach of the Year. And Scott May was named the consensus Player of the Year. In total, Indiana had three All-Americans— May, Kent Benson, and Quinn Buckner. In addition, Benson was named the Most Outstanding Player of the Final Four.

Shortly after the NCAA Tournament, Indiana had four players drafted into the National Basketball Association (NBA). May went second to the Chicago Bulls, Buckner went seventh to the Milwaukee Bucks, and Bob Wilkerson went eleventh to the Seattle SuperSonics. In addition, Abernethy was a third-round pick of the Los Angeles Lakers. Benson was just a junior in 1975–76. He went on to be drafted first overall by the Bucks in 1977. Benson had the longest NBA career of any of the 1975–76 Hoosiers. He played 11 NBA seasons.

with his defense on UCLA's All-American forward, Richard Washington. Abernethy also contributed 16 points on 7-of-8 shooting. Benson paced Indiana with 14 points, while Wilkerson had 19 rebounds. It was the most rebounds ever for a Hoosiers guard. Indiana won the game 65–51.

Michigan was the only team standing between Indiana and a perfect season. The Hoosiers had faced their Big Ten rival twice during the regular season. Indiana won both early meetings, but only by a total of 11 points. And one of those wins came in overtime.

The third matchup—for the NCAA Tournament title—did not get off to a good start for Indiana. Wilkerson suffered a concussion in the third minute of the game. He was unable to return. Without their point guard, the Hoosiers trailed at halftime 35–29.

In the final 20 minutes, though, Indiana regained its form. Knight once called the second half "the 20-minute

segment that we played the best basketball that we played at any time during the course of the season." After scoring only one point in the first half, Buckner stepped up in the second half. He scored 15 points after the break. He also finished the game with eight rebounds, five steals, and four assists.

And once again, May and Benson controlled the paint. May finished with 26 points, while Benson had 25. With 10:15 left, the game was tied at 51–51. From that point on, the Hoosiers outscored the Wolverines 35–17. The Hoosiers went on to win 86–68.

Knight's team had achieved its only goal. The Hoosiers did not just win. They did not just dominate. They were perfect.

[11]

Indiana University was founded in 1824.
The first Indiana men's basketball team
played in 1901.

2

THE EARLY YEARS

D R. JAMES NAISMITH INVENTED BASKETBALL IN 1891 AT A SCHOOL IN MASSACHUSETTS. TEN YEARS LATER, ON FEBRUARY 8, 1901, THE INDIANA HOOSIERS BASKETBALL PROGRAM BEGAN. FROM THE BEGINNING INDIANA PLAYED IN THE BIG TEN CONFERENCE. HOWEVER, IT WAS KNOWN AS THE WESTERN CONFERENCE UNTIL 1917–18.

In 1901, a team of six players (and 100 fans) took a train to Indianapolis. The team's opponent was the Butler Bulldogs. The Hoosiers lost the game 20–17. Still, the fans enjoyed the exciting, hard-fought contest.

Thirteen days later, Indiana and Butler again squared off. The Bulldogs won that game, too, 24–20. Indiana then lost its first meeting with its in-state archrival, the Purdue Boilermakers. But in its fourth game, Indiana finally notched a victory. The 26–17 win against the Wabash Little Giants brought the Hoosiers' first season to a close.

HOOSIERS

Indiana has used the nickname Hoosiers ever since debuting its basketball program in 1901. The nickname is actually the same as the state nickname. Indiana is known as "The Hoosier State," though the origin of the nickname is unclear. It might be a reference to Indiana pioneers saying "Who's here?" when someone knocked on their cabin door. Another theory is that Indiana residents were excellent at silencing their opponents in battle. As a result, they were known as "hushers," which in turn became "Hoosiers." Many theories exist, but nobody knows the definite origin of "Hoosiers."

Indiana's first 16 basketball seasons did not produce a lot of victories. The Hoosiers won just 43 percent of their games between their first season and the 1915–16 season. In only five of those seasons did Indiana win more games than it lost.

However, the Hoosiers began to enjoy success in 1916–17. Starting that season, they finished with a winning record in five straight years. During that stretch, Everett Dean became the first All-America player at Indiana as a senior in 1920–21. He played center, even though he was just 6-feet tall. That was tall in those days, but today centers are typically much taller. Dean averaged 10.7 points per game as a senior.

In 1924, Dean returned to Indiana—as the Hoosiers' coach. In Dean's second season in charge, the Hoosiers tied for first place in the Big Ten. It was their first conference championship. In Dean's fourth season, Indiana finished with its best record to that point, going 15–2. Dean coached the team through the 1937–38 season. The Hoosiers finished with a winning record in 10 of his 14 seasons.

Branch McCracken, one of Dean's former All-America players, took over as Indiana's coach in 1938–39. McCracken would coach the Hoosiers for 24 seasons. He won nearly 68 percent of his games, finishing with a 364–174 record.

McCracken's arrival as Indiana's coach also coincided with the beginning of the NCAA Tournament. The Hoosiers did not qualify for the inaugural tournament in McCracken's first season. But in his second season, in 1940, Indiana was invited to participate in the tournament.

There were only eight teams in the NCAA Tournament that year. So after defeating Springfield and Duquesne, Indiana was in the final. The Hoosiers' opponent, the Kansas Jayhawks, was one of the legendary programs in the sport. But All-American Marv Huffman scored 12 points, leading the Hoosiers to a 60–42 victory.

The Hoosiers' second championship came in the 1952–53 season. Don Schlundt, a 6-foot-9 center, was Indiana's best player. Schlundt was named an All-American as a sophomore, a junior, and a senior. He was

BILL GARRETT: A HOOSIERS PIONEER

In 1948, Indiana's Bill Garrett became the Big Ten Conference's first black varsity athlete. He led the Hoosiers in scoring and rebounding in all three of his varsity seasons. As a senior, Garrett was named an All-American. He averaged 13.1 points per game that season, in 1950–51. He also broke the Hoosiers' all-time scoring record.

THE EARLY YEARS

THE TITLE TEAM

Indiana's 1952–53 championship team had two star players. Center Don Schlundt was known as "Mr. Inside." He dominated the paint for the Hoosiers, averaging 25.4 points and 10.0 rebounds per game. Guard Bob Leonard was "Mr. Outside." He averaged 16.3 points per game.

Schlundt and Leonard had plenty of help, too. Forward Charles Kraak was a rebounding machine, averaging 10.7 per game. The Hoosiers' other starting forward was Dick Farley. He led the Big Ten with a 44.3 percent field-goal percentage that season. The other starting guard was Burke Scott. The sophomore was a tenacious defender and a strong ball-handler.

As a team, the 1952–53 Hoosiers won the first outright Big Ten title in school history. They also were the first Indiana team to become the unanimous number-one ranked team in the country. And, of course, they were the second Indiana team to win a national title.

the first three-time All-American in Hoosiers' history.

As a sophomore in 1952–53, Schlundt led Indiana to a 23–3 record. His biggest game might have been against the Notre Dame Fighting Irish in the Elite Eight. Schlundt scored 41 points in the victory. Then he scored 30 points in the 1953 NCAA Tournament title game against Kansas. Bobby Leonard made the winning foul shot with 27 seconds left. Charles Kraak added 17 points as Indiana won 69–68.

McCracken's teams never made another Final Four. That said, the Hoosiers had plenty of star players during McCracken's final 12 years as coach.

Forward-center Archie Dees was the Big Ten's Most Valuable Player (MVP) in 1957 and 1958. He was also a two-time All-American, as were Walt Bellamy (1960, 1961) and Jimmy Rayl (1962, 1963). Then in 1964–65, two identical twins were each named All-Americans

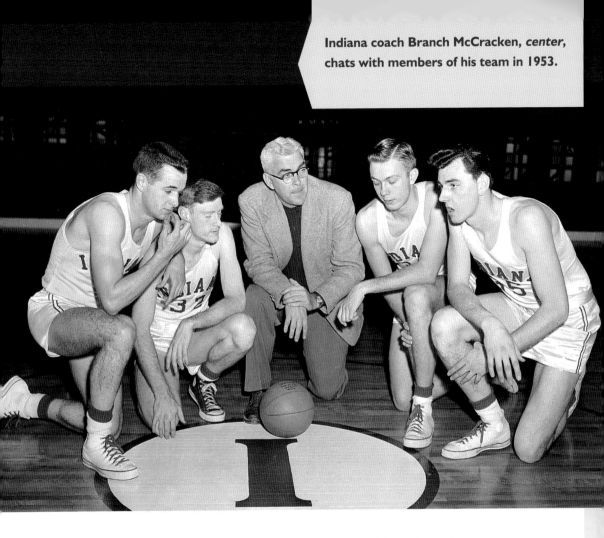

for Indiana. Tom Van Arsdale averaged 18.4 points and 8.5 rebounds per game that season. And Dick Van Arsdale contributed 17.2 points and 8.7 rebounds per game.

After McCracken left, Indiana had a couple of tough seasons in the late 1960s. The Hoosiers won only eight games in 1965–66. In 1968–69 and 1969–70, the Hoosiers' combined record was just 16–32. And from 1966 to 1970, the team did not have a single player selected for the All-America team. But fortunately for the Hoosiers, "The General" was about to take charge.

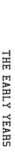

THE EARLY YEARS

Coach Bobby Knight brought his fiery temper—and lots of success—to Indiana beginning in 1971–72.

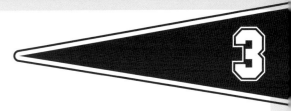

3

KNIGHT TIME

APRIL 1, 1971, MARKED A NEW ERA IN HOOSIERS BASKETBALL. ON THAT DAY, BOBBY KNIGHT TOOK OVER AS INDIANA'S HEAD COACH. SOON AFTER, THE SCHOOL OPENED ITS NEW BASKETBALL ARENA, ASSEMBLY HALL.

Knight, the former head coach at Army, was known as "The General." He was a hard-nosed coach who preached discipline and toughness. On offense, he stressed unselfish play and smart shot selection. On defense, his teams played a physical man-to-man scheme.

The Hoosiers won 17 games in Knight's first season. They got consistently better over the next four years. And as they did, the Hoosiers began to take control of the Big Ten. In Knight's first five seasons, the Hoosiers finished first in the conference four times.

In 1973, Indiana reached the Final Four for the first time since 1953. Center Steve Downing and forward John Ritter led the way. The Hoosiers ultimately lost 70–59 to the UCLA Bruins in the Final Four. Yet the program was officially back. Knight was honored as the Big Ten's Coach of the Year. Downing was an All-American and the Big Ten MVP. No Hoosier had been named league MVP in 15 years.

Two years later, the Hoosiers took another step forward. The 1974–75 team was a dominant force. Indiana began the season with a 53-point win over the Tennessee Tech Golden Eagles. The Hoosiers then won three straight games against the Kansas Jayhawks, the Kentucky Wildcats, and the Notre Dame Fighting Irish. All three of those teams were ranked in the top 20 at the time.

Indiana sat at 11–0 entering Big Ten play. The Hoosiers then dominated several of their biggest rivals. They defeated the Michigan State Spartans by 52 points. They won by 33 points against the Purdue Boilermakers. And they defeated the Michigan Wolverines twice, by a combined 40 points.

GEORGE McGINNIS

Prior to Bobby Knight's first season, Indiana had lost several key players from its roster. The most significant loss was George McGinnis. The sophomore forward decided to go pro after just one varsity season with Indiana. During that one season, McGinnis averaged 29.9 points and 14.7 rebounds per game. He led the Big Ten in both scoring and rebounding. In fact, his scoring average was a Hoosiers' record. McGinnis was named an All-American in his only season with the Hoosiers. He went on to become a three-time All-Star in the American Basketball Association and the NBA.

However, in an 83–82 win over Purdue, leading scorer Scott May fractured his hand. The Hoosiers were largely without May going forward. He had played a few minutes in the final game of the regular season. But his arm was in a cast, and it was wrapped in foam rubber. Still, Indiana was 29–0 entering the NCAA Tournament. In the first two rounds of the NCAA Tournament, May played a total of just four minutes. And he did not score in either contest. Still, Knight decided to start May against Kentucky in the Elite Eight.

The decision backfired. May struggled through seven minutes of action. The Wildcats were physical with the Hoosiers and came away with a 92–90 upset. Sophomore center Kent Benson led Indiana with 33 points and 23 rebounds—both career highs. But he left the court in tears as the Hoosiers' dreams of a perfect season ended.

"It's been an enjoyable year," Knight said to the press. "We'll be back some day."

That day, of course, came just one year later. The Hoosiers returned to the 1976 NCAA Tournament undefeated. And this time they completed the march to perfection, finishing 32–0.

The quest to repeat as champions did not go well, however. The Hoosiers scuffled to a 14–13 finish in 1976–77. They did not have May, Quinn Buckner, Bob Wilkerson, or Tom Abernethy, all of whom were now in the NBA. Benson, now a senior, was named an All-American for the third straight season. But his stellar play was not nearly enough to carry the team.

NIT CHAMPS

In 1979, Indiana missed the NCAA Tournament for the second time in three seasons. However, the Hoosiers went on to win the National Invitation Tournament (NIT) that year. They defeated their rival Purdue to win the crown. The final score was Hoosiers 53, Boilermakers 52. Indiana's Butch Carter hit the game-winning jump shot with five seconds left. It was the first, and only, NIT title in Hoosiers' history through 2013.

Indiana missed the NCAA Tournament in 1977 and 1979 but was back in a big way in 1981. Sophomore point guard Isiah Thomas was the star on that team. He averaged 16.0 points and 5.8 assists per game that season. The team's other four starters all averaged between 9.2 and 12.2 points per game. They were forwards Ted Kitchel (9.2) and Landon Turner (9.5), guard Randy Wittman (10.4), and center Ray Tolbert (12.2).

The 1980–81 season did not begin in impressive fashion. At the start of Big Ten play, Indiana's record was just 6–5. Yet the Hoosiers had won five in a row by the time the NCAA Tournament rolled around.

KNIGHT TIME

ISIAH THOMAS

The Detroit Pistons selected Isiah Thomas with the second pick in the 1981 NBA Draft. Thomas went on to become one of the greatest point guards in NBA history. He made 12 All-Star teams in his 13 NBA seasons. He led Detroit to two NBA championships, and he was named the NBA Finals MVP in one of them. Thomas was inducted into the Naismith Memorial Basketball Hall of Fame in 2000.

"I went to Indiana University, played under Coach Knight," Thomas said in his induction speech. "Had a wonderful career there."

Thomas is one of the rare players in hoops history to win Most Outstanding Player of the Final Four (1981) and NBA Finals MVP (1990).

To win the title, they needed to win five more games in a row. And that's just what they did. The third-seeded Hoosiers began by routing the Maryland Terrapins 99–64. After two more double-digit wins, Indiana was back in the Final Four. The Louisiana State University (LSU) Tigers led the Hoosiers 30–27 at halftime. But Indiana dominated in the second half. Turner finished with 20 points and eight rebounds. Thomas added 14 points in the Hoosiers' 67–49 victory.

The national championship game was a rematch between Indiana and the North Carolina Tar Heels. The teams had met about three months earlier on the Tar Heels' home court. The Hoosiers lost that game 65–56 back in December. But this time, they got their revenge.

Indiana won its fourth NCAA title with a 63–50 victory. Wittman's jump shot at the first-half buzzer gave the Hoosiers their first lead by a score of 27–26.

"That was the most important play of the game," Thomas said later that night. "It gave us momentum." Thomas was the fuel behind that momentum in the second half. The sophomore star scored 19 of his 23 points after halftime. Backup guard Jim Thomas chipped in 16 points, while Turner added 12.

At the time, the Hoosiers' nine losses were the most ever for an NCAA champion. That served as a contrast to the 1975–76 team. That squad had set the record for most wins ever by an NCAA champion with 32 victories. Nevertheless, both teams were champions. And when it came to winning titles, Knight was not done yet.

[25]

KNIGHT TIME

Indiana guard Steve Alford brings the ball up the court during a 1987 game against Northwestern.

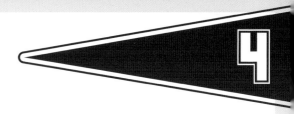

KNIGHT RISES, KNIGHT FALLS

BY THE TIME INDIANA RETURNED TO THE COURT IN 1981–82, ISIAH THOMAS WAS ALREADY IN THE NBA. HOOSIERS FANS WONDERED WHEN THEY EVER WOULD LOVE ANOTHER PLAYER AS MUCH AS THOMAS. WELL, THEY DID NOT HAVE TO WAIT LONG.

In 1983, Steve Alford arrived on campus. The sweet-shooting guard had been named Indiana's "Mr. Basketball" as a high school senior. He averaged 37.7 points per game in his senior season in high school. Alford made an immediate impact at Indiana. He led the team in scoring in all four of his seasons. He was named an All-American during his junior and senior seasons. But it was his senior season that truly made him an Indiana legend.

As a senior, Alford led the 1986–87 Hoosiers to a 23–2 start. The team then dropped two of its final three regular-season games. Despite the late-season slump, the Hoosiers still received a number-one seed in the NCAA Tournament.

Between Alford, center Dean Garrett, forward Daryl Thomas, guard Keith Smart, and swingman Rick Calloway, the Hoosiers showcased tremendous individual offense on the way to the Final Four. A different player led the team in scoring in each of the first three games.

In the Final Four, the Hoosiers' backcourt simply took over. First came a 97–93 win against the University of Nevada-Las Vegas Rebels. Alford scored 33 points, while Smart added 14. Then came the NCAA Tournament title game—a 74–73 victory over the Syracuse Orangemen. Alford scored a game-high 23 points, while Smart was named Most Outstanding Player of the Final Four. Against Syracuse, Smart had 21 points, including the four biggest points in the game.

In the final minute, Syracuse led 73–70 when Smart drove the length of the court for a short jump shot. Orangemen forward Derrick Coleman then missed a free throw, giving the ball back to the Hoosiers. On Indiana's final possession, Alford could not get open. The Hoosiers instead worked the ball into Thomas, who was covered by Coleman. So Thomas passed the ball back to Smart, who rose up for a tough 17-foot

STEVE ALFORD

Steve Alford was one of Bobby Knight's all-time favorite players at Indiana. Knight once said of the Hoosiers' star: "He's gotten more out of his abilities offensively than anybody I've seen play college basketball." After leaving Indiana, Alford enjoyed a short NBA career. He took over as head coach at UCLA in 2013.

Dean Garrett (22) congratulates Indiana teammate Keith Smart (23) during the 1987 NCAA title game.

jump shot from the left baseline. It swished through the basket with just four seconds left.

Syracuse had one last desperation pass. But Smart intercepted the heave. With that, Indiana had won its fifth NCAA championship. Even the normally grumpy Bobby Knight had reason to smile.

[29]

Indiana's Keith Smart cuts down the net after the Hoosiers defeated the Syracuse Orangemen to win the 1987 NCAA title.

"I'm happy as [heck] that we won," Knight said afterward. "I'm happy because I think we have great fans, and great people, and they enjoy it. It's great for them."

Indiana was back in the Final Four in 1992. That team was led by star junior Calbert Cheaney. The lefty swingman averaged 17.6 points per game that season. He scored 23 points in the Elite Eight as the Hoosiers upset top-seeded UCLA. In the Final Four, Indiana led defending champion Duke 42–37 at halftime. However, the Blue Devils came back in the second half to win 81–78. Cheaney was held to 11 points. It was the Hoosiers' first loss in a Final Four game since 1973.

In Cheaney's senior season, the Hoosiers had another shot at the Final Four. They faced the second-seeded Kansas Jayhawks in the Elite Eight. Cheaney scored 22 points, and senior guard Greg Graham had 23. But the Hoosiers lost 83–77. Despite the loss, Cheaney was named an All-American for the third straight season. This time, he also was honored as the Player of the Year in college basketball.

That was the last time the Hoosiers reached the Elite Eight under Knight's guidance. In fact, the next season—1993–94—was the final time Knight even reached the Sweet 16 at Indiana.

Knight's career at Indiana featured some of the highest highs and lowest lows. He won three NCAA championships with the Hoosiers. He brought the program to incredible heights. Yet his temper also led to numerous controversies throughout his 29 seasons at Indiana. And ultimately, those issues led to his dismissal from the university.

CALBERT CHEANEY

Calbert Cheaney left Indiana as the school's all-time leading scorer with 2,613 career points. That broke Steve Alford's previous record of 2,438 points. In fact, it broke the Big Ten career scoring record. Through the 2012–13 season, no player in Big Ten history had scored more career points than Cheaney.

BAD BEHAVIOR

Bobby Knight had a long history of being physical with his players, shouting at officials and members of the media, and engaging in altercations with opposing fans. In 1979, Knight was convicted of hitting a policeman in Puerto Rico. In 1981, an LSU fan claimed Knight stuffed him into a trash can. Four years later, Knight threw a chair across the court to protest officiating in a game against Purdue. Then in 1991, Knight barred a female reporter from his locker room. Three years later, he head-butted a Hoosiers player while screaming at him on the bench. And then in 1999, Knight was investigated for allegedly choking a man at a restaurant. "I do dumb things sometimes," Knight once said.

However, on the court Knight won 899 games—the third most by any coach through 2013—and is in the Naismith Basketball Hall of Fame.

The final straw for Knight at Indiana came in 2000. In March of that year, one of Knight's former players accused Knight of choking him at a practice back in 1997. As a result, Knight was suspended and fined by the university. Knight was now facing a "zero-tolerance policy." Indiana president Myles Brand warned that if there was one more incident, Knight would be fired.

That incident took place on September 7, 2000. A student named Kent Harvey allegedly addressed the coach, "Hey, Knight. What's up?" Knight apparently grabbed the student's arm and lectured him about manners. Three days later, Knight was fired. Brand called Knight's history of incidents "a pattern of unacceptable behavior."

Knight was criticized, fined, suspended, or reprimanded for many incidents during his three decades at Indiana. When he was ultimately fired, many Hoosiers fans were upset. An estimated 4,000 students marched

Bobby Knight, shown in 2000, was fired after violating the school's zero tolerance policy later that year.

outside Brand's residence in protest. But despite their pleas, Knight was not coming back.

The Hoosiers—and their fans—had to move on.

INDIANA UNIVERSITY NCAA BASKETBALL CHAMPIONS 1976

Die-hard Indiana basketball fans cheer on the Hoosiers during a 2002 game at Assembly Hall.

THE NEW HOOSIERS

INDIANA FIRED BOBBY KNIGHT ON SEPTEMBER 10, 2000. THE HOOSIERS' SEASON WAS SET TO BEGIN ON NOVEMBER 14. IN ADDITION, SOME PLAYERS AND FANS WERE QUITE ANGRY ABOUT KNIGHT'S FIRING. SO THE UNIVERSITY NEEDED TO ACT QUICKLY.

Three days later, on September 13, Indiana promoted assistant coach Mike Davis to replace Knight. At first, several Hoosiers players considered transferring. But ultimately all 12 returning players stayed with the program. And the continuity paid off almost immediately.

In 2001–02, the Hoosiers were 20–11 heading into the NCAA Tournament. They had not won five games in a row all season. Yet that's what they did when it mattered most.

The most dramatic win came in the Sweet 16 against the Duke Blue Devils. The Hoosiers trailed by 17 points in the first half. But they rallied and led by four points in the final seconds. Duke had a chance to tie when star guard Jason

Williams was fouled on a made three-pointer. But Williams missed the free throw and Duke could not convert the offensive rebound.

With one more win over the Kent State Golden Flashes, Indiana was back in the Final Four for the first time since 1992. The Hoosiers' three-point shooting was again excellent against the Oklahoma Sooners. Seven different Indiana players made a three-pointer. As a team, the Hoosiers made 8-of-13 from three-point range. Reserve forward Jeff Newton poured in a career-high 19 points as Indiana won the game 73–64.

The dream run finally ended in the championship game against the Maryland Terrapins. Indiana only led for eight seconds and shot just 35 percent from the field. The Hoosiers also committed 16 turnovers in the 64–52 defeat.

"I think this was a tremendous accomplishment this season," Davis said. "I don't think losing in the final takes anything away from our run. I'm very proud of our basketball team."

Davis coached Indiana for four more seasons. However, the 2001–02 season was the high point. He never again led Indiana past the second

A. J. GUYTON

The 2000–01 season was not just about replacing Bobby Knight. The Hoosiers also had to replace their best player. A. J. Guyton, a sweet-shooting guard, graduated in 2000. Guyton left as the all-time leading three-point shooter in Indiana history. He made 283 career three-pointers. He also finished his career with 2,100 points—fourth-most in Indiana history through 2013.

Indiana's Jared Jeffries, *right*, battles for the ball with Maryland's Chris Wilcox during the 2002 NCAA title game.

round of the NCAA Tournament. In 2004 and 2005, the Hoosiers missed the NCAA Tournament altogether. It was the first time that Indiana missed the tournament in back-to-back years since 1971 and 1972. Even worse, the Hoosiers finished just 14–15 in 2003–04. It was their first losing season since 1969–70.

Kelvin Sampson replaced Davis on the Indiana bench after the 2005–06 season. Sampson lasted less than two full seasons with the Hoosiers. He was penalized for various NCAA violations. As a result, Sampson resigned 26 games into his second season.

That 2007–08 season was going well, too. The Hoosiers were 22–4 at the time of Sampson's resignation. And they had their first All-America players in six years—freshman guard Eric Gordon and senior center D. J. White. Dan Dakich took over as interim head coach. However, Dakich only held the job for seven games. Four of those games were losses. The

Hoosiers lost their first game in the Big Ten Tournament. Then they lost in their first NCAA Tournament game.

The program was in need of a new start after that. Indiana got just that when the school hired former Marquette coach Tom Crean on April 2, 2008. With that hiring came a new and improved era for the Hoosiers. But it started off slowly.

In all, Indiana had only one returning scholarship player in 2008–09. Seven eligible players had left the program before Crean's first season. Gordon entered the NBA Draft. Two others transferred. Four more had been dismissed from the team. And the Hoosiers also lost two scholarships due to NCAA penalties. So it was little surprise when Indiana went just 6–25 in 2008–09. At one point, Crean described his team as being in "crisis mode." In addition, Assembly Hall was no longer selling out.

Things gradually improved. The Hoosiers went 10–21 in 2009–10. They then improved to 12–20 in 2010–11. Crean was starting to add

INDIANA BASKETBALL

The people of Indiana are some of the most passionate basketball fans in the world. The state's passion for high school basketball was showcased in the classic 1986 movie *Hoosiers*. The state's passion for college basketball can be seen in the arenas of any of its major college basketball teams, including Butler, Indiana, Notre Dame, Purdue, and Valparaiso. No team, however, is as popular as the Hoosiers. As Bobby Knight once said, "Basketball may have been invented in Massachusetts, but it was made for Indiana."

FACING KENTUCKY

In the 2011–12 season, two of Indiana's biggest games came against Kentucky. In the regular season, Indiana defeated the top-ranked Wildcats 73–72. Forward Christian Watford hit a game-winning three-pointer at the buzzer. The play is known around Indiana as "The Shot." In some ways, it signaled a message to the college basketball world: The Indiana Hoosiers were back. "It proved that we could be a legit team," Watford said in 2013.

The teams also met in the Sweet 16. The Wildcats got their revenge in that one, ending the Hoosiers' season. Watford led Indiana with 27 points in the 102–90 loss. Kentucky went on to win the national championship. It was the Wildcats' eighth NCAA title. Through 2013, UCLA led all schools with 11 NCAA championships. Kentucky was second with eight while Indiana and North Carolina were tied for third with five NCAA titles each.

some legitimate talent. Sophomore forward Christian Watford led the 2010–11 team in scoring. Guards Victor Oladipo and Jordan Hulls were promising young players, as well.

In the 2011–12 season, the Hoosiers debuted one of the top freshmen in the country. Cody Zeller, a 7-foot center, had been "Mr. Basketball" in Indiana as a high school senior. He arrived on campus and the Hoosiers immediately got better. Indiana improved to 27–9. Zeller led the team with 15.6 points and 6.6 rebounds per game as a freshman. And the Hoosiers returned to the NCAA Tournament for the first time since 2008.

The next season, 2012–13, the Hoosiers took their success a step further. Led by Oladipo and Zeller, Indiana began the season ranked number one in the country. They won their first nine games. And they won 20 of their first 22 games. At 27–6, the Hoosiers were a number-one seed in the NCAA

Indiana guard Victor Oladipo, *left*, and center Cody Zeller celebrate after a win in the 2013 NCAA Tournament.

Tournament. The team disappointed after that, however. The Syracuse Orange defeated the Hoosiers in the Sweet 16. Still, the season was generally viewed as a positive step for Indiana.

"This group has done things that have not been done at Indiana in a long time," Crean said. "They made it a big-time place again."

The Indiana Hoosiers play their first basketball game on February 8. Butler defeats the Hoosiers 20–17 in Indianapolis.

Everett Dean becomes the first All-American for the Hoosiers.

Indiana earns a share of the Big Ten Conference championship. It is the first league title in school history.

The Hoosiers defeat Kansas for the first NCAA title in school history on March 30.

Indiana's Bill Garrett becomes the first black athlete to play a varsity sport in the Big Ten.

1901 1921 1926 1940 1948

Indiana defeats North Carolina 63–50 to win another NCAA championship on March 30. Isiah Thomas scores 23 points to lead the Hoosiers.

In one of his most famous incidents, Knight throws a chair across the court during a February 23 game against Purdue. Knight is suspended for one game.

Keith Smart makes a jump shot with four seconds left, giving Indiana a 74–73 victory over Syracuse in the NCAA Tournament championship game on March 30.

Knight becomes the youngest coach in college basketball history to reach 600 career wins. He retires with 899 wins.

Calbert Cheaney becomes the all-time leading scorer in the history of Indiana—and the Big Ten.

1981 1985 1987 1993 1993

Indiana defeats
Kansas 69-68 on
March 18 to win
its second national
championship. Bob
Leonard's late free
throw provides the
winning point.

Bobby Knight begins
his job as Indiana's
head basketball coach
on April 1.

Indiana plays its first
game in its brand new
arena, Assembly Hall,
on December 1. The
Hoosiers defeat Ball
State 84–77.

Indiana advances to
the Final Four with
a 72–65 win over
Kentucky. In just his
second season, Knight
comes within two
wins of a national
championship.

Indiana's 86–68
victory over Michigan
on March 29 gives
the Hoosiers their
third national
championship
and clinches an
undefeated season.

1953   1971   1971   1973   1976

Knight is fired as
Indiana's coach on
September 10, three
days after allegedly
grabbing a student's
arm and lecturing him
about manners.

Under second-year
coach Mike Davis,
Indiana loses the
NCAA Tournament
title game against
Maryland on April 1.

Indiana coach Kelvin
Sampson resigns 26
games into his second
season due to NCAA
violations.

Tom Crean takes over
as Indiana's coach
on April 2 but has
only one scholarship
player on the roster in
2008–09.

Indiana begins the
2012–13 season
ranked first in the
nation. It is the first
time the Hoosiers
are ranked number
one since 1992–93.
However, they lose in
the Sweet 16.

2000   2002   2008   2008   2013

QUICK STATS

PROGRAM INFO
Indiana University Hoosiers (1901–)

NCAA TOURNAMENT FINALS
(WINS IN BOLD)
1940, **1953**, **1976**, **1981**, **1987**, 2002

OTHER ACHIEVEMENTS
Final Fours: 8
NCAA Tournaments: 37

KEY PLAYERS
(POSITION(S); YEARS WITH TEAM)
Steve Alford (G; 1983–87)
Walt Bellamy (C; 1958–61)
Kent Benson (C; 1973–77)
Quinn Buckner (G; 1972–76)
Calbert Cheaney (F; 1989–93)
Archie Dees (G; 1955–58)
Bill Garrett (F; 1948–51)
Eric Gordon (G; 2007–08)
Steve Green (F; 1972–75)
Marv Huffman (G; 1937–40)
Jared Jeffries (F; 2000–02)
Scott May (F; 1973–76)
Branch McCracken (G; 1927–30)

George McGinnis (F; 1970–71)
Victor Oladipo (G; 2010–13)
Jimmy Rayl (G; 1960–63)
Don Schlundt (C; 1951–55)
Isiah Thomas (G; 1979–81)
Mike Woodson (F; 1976–80)
Cody Zeller (C; 2011–13)

KEY COACHES
Branch McCracken (1938–43; 1946–65):
 364–174; 9–2 (NCAA Tournament)
Bobby Knight (1971–2000):
 659–242; 42–21 (NCAA
 Tournament)

HOME ARENA
Assembly Hall (1971–)

* All statistics through 2012–13 season

Even after winning the 1976 national championship, Bobby Knight was busy. "I'm not paid to relax," he said. "I'll be on the train tomorrow—recruiting."

The 1975–76 Hoosiers are considered one of the greatest teams in college basketball history. They defeated their five NCAA Tournament opponents by a total of 66 points. The 1980–81 Hoosiers, meanwhile, are not regarded as highly as the 1975–76 team. Yet they defeated their five tournament opponents by a whopping 113 points.

Calbert Cheaney was the first left-handed player Bob Knight had at Indiana. Cheaney joined the Hoosiers in 1989, nearly 20 years after Knight became the school's head coach.

In the 1917–18 season, Indiana moved into a new arena called Men's Gymnasium. Right away, the Hoosiers fans complained about the gym's wooden backboards. The fans could not see the action through the wood. So in 1917, Indiana became the first school in the country to play with glass backboards.

One of Bobby Knight's most memorable jabs at the media was: "All of us learn to write in second grade. Most of us go on to other things."

GLOSSARY

All-American
A player chosen as one of the best amateurs in the country in a particular activity.

amateur
An athlete who is not paid to compete.

conference
In sports, a group of teams that plays each other each season.

consensus
Unanimous agreement.

draft
A system used by professional sports leagues to select new players in order to spread incoming talent among all teams. The NBA Draft is held each June.

interim
Temporary.

rivals
Opponents that bring out great emotion in a team, its fans, and its players.

scheme
A system of play.

scholarship
Financial assistance awarded to students to help them pay for school. Top athletes earn scholarships to represent a college through its sports teams.

seed
In basketball, a ranking system used for tournaments. The best teams earn a number-one seed.

upset
A result where the supposedly worse team defeats the supposedly better team.

varsity
The main team in a given sport that represents a school.

FOR MORE INFORMATION

FURTHER READING

DeCock, Luke. *Great Teams in College Basketball History*. Chicago, IL: Heinemann-Raintree, 2005.

Hiner, Jason. *Indiana University Basketball Encyclopedia*. Champaign, IL: Sports Publishing, 2005.

Laskowski, John. *Tales from the Indiana Hoosiers Locker Room: A Collection of the Greatest Indiana Basketball Stories Ever Told*. New York: Sports Publishing, 2012.

WEB LINKS

To learn more about the Indiana Hoosiers, visit ABDO Publishing Company online at **www.abdopublishing.com**. Web sites about the Hoosiers are featured on our Book Links page. These links are routinely monitored and updated to provide the most current information available.

PLACES TO VISIT

Assembly Hall
1001 E. 17th Street
Bloomington, IN 47408
812-855-4848
www.iuhoosiers.com/facilities/ind-facilities-assembly.html

This has been the Hoosiers' home arena since 1971. Assembly Hall is known for being one of the loudest college basketball arenas in the country. Tours are available when the Hoosiers are not playing.

Indiana Basketball Hall of Fame
One Hall of Fame Court
New Castle, IN 47362
765-529-1891
www.hoopshall.com

This shrine to basketball in the state of Indiana honors some of the greatest players, coaches, and moments in Hoosiers history. Among the former Indiana legends inducted into the Indiana Basketball Hall of Fame are Bobby Knight, Kent Benson, and Steve Alford.

INDEX

ABOUT THE AUTHOR

Drew Silverman is a sportswriter based in Philadelphia, Pennsylvania. He graduated from Syracuse University in 2004. He then worked as a sportswriter and editor at ESPN's headquarters in Bristol, Connecticut, before returning back home to Philadelphia. After several years as the sports editor for *The Bulletin* newspaper, he began working for NBC Sports as an editorial content manager. He currently lives in Philadelphia with his wife and their dog, Samson.